SELF-MOTIVATION, DETERMINATION AND SHARING THE KEY
ROLES TO BEATING THE ODDS IN LIFE

WIN THE COURT

UNKNOWN STUDENT-ATHLETE

A STORY WRITTEN BY
Dorian Dunson II

Win the Court

COPYRIGHT 2018

All Rights Reserved

ISBN: 9781724177315

ASIN: 1724177311

Printed in the United States of America

Cover and Interior Design: Canva.com

Acknowledgments

Putting this book together assimilates a winning mindset and personal accomplishments. I have many people to thank for assistance along the way: my wife, parents, brother, coaches, friends, teammates, mentors, teachers, facility of universities, and business associates who have contributed to my life in one way or another.

There are a few people that I would want to give a special thanks. First, I would like to thank the Lord, without you none of this would have been possible. I would like to thank my wife: without my better half, I would not be the person I am today. You continue to push me to strive for excellence. You are the backbone of our family and what you do never goes unnoticed. Next, I would like to thank my brother for always being there for me and supporting my dreams and goals. Then I would like to thank my parents for supporting me through everything and teaching me how to become a man of integrity and learning how to serve the Lord. Last but not least, I would like to thank everyone who has helped me make this book possible including my best friend. Without your friendship and guidance as a mentor, it has allowed me to never let anything or anyone stop me from my dreams. It's been a wonderful journey to let people know that no obstacle that has come in my way has defeated me especially when you are willing to try. You can be anything you want to be if you put your mind to it.

To my wife, family, friends, and fans, without whom I wouldn't be where I am today. Thank you for teaching me the power of words, and believing that anything is possible.

– Dodie Dunson, II.

Introduction

Win the Court: Self-motivation, determination, sharing the key roles to beating the odds in life examines the art of educational success and creating opportunities to help shape the person you are and who you want to become. This story is about a person overcoming a learning disability. After struggling in the classroom his whole life, he started a journey to accomplish his goals and dreams. Dunson was diagnosed with a severe form of dyslexia. He has not allowed his learning disability to hinder his academic success; however, to overcome it, he

6

dedicated himself to studying and working hard. This book will encourage others to press forward; we hope it motivates you to follow your own path in life and pursue your purpose.

Dorian Dunson II is currently a women's assistant basketball coach. He has served at multiple institutional universities, colleges, and high schools throughout his coaching career. Dunson's academic success has helped shaped his journey; he earned his Associates of Arts degree (A.A.) in General Studies from Vincennes University, a Bachelor's of Science (B.S.) in Social Work from Bradley University, and a Master's of Science degree in Education (M.S. Ed.) from Southern Illinois University Edwardsville.

Contents

Front Cover
01

Copy Right
02

Acknowledgements
03

Thankful For
05

Introduction
06

Contents
08

Chapter 1–Chasing a Dream
10

Chapter 2 - Knowing Yourself
18

Chapter 3–Creating Opportunities

8

29

Chapter 4–Self Motivation
37
Iowa State University
38
Vincennes University
43
Bradley University
53

Chapter 5–Dunson Key Principles
67

1

Childhood
Chasing a Dream

"Don't ever let someone tell you that you can't do something. Not even me. You got a dream, you got to protect it. When people can't do something themselves, they're going to tell you that you can't do it. You want something go get it. Period."

— Will Smith

Chapter One: Childhood – Chasing a Dream

My name is Dorian David Dunson, Jr. Most people know me as "Dodie" and this is my story. I was born in Gardena, California but was raised in the small town of Bloomington, Illinois a few hours right outside of Chicago. Bloomington is a

blue-collar town known as the home of State Farm Insurance, Country Company, and the Nestle confections

factory. As a kid, I made a promise to myself that one day that I would do whatever it took to become a college basketball player, graduate from college and play professional basketball. When I was in kindergarten, my father introduced me to the game.

When I was very little, I remember my parents buying me a plastic basketball hoop for Christmas, and I thought it was the best gift a kid could ever receive. I was blessed to have both my parents and they were hard working. My mother worked in the corporate world at State Farm and my father worked at a community center with intercity youth. Working at Western Avenue Community Center he created several programs aimed to help youth learn and grow as individuals. My father played college basketball at Parkland College in Champaign, IL and went on to play in the summer pro leagues in California when I was an infant. My father had professional basketball opportunities but was cut during training camps by a few NBA franchises, the Los Angeles Clippers and the Washington Bullets, now called the Washington Wizards.

My Parents instilled in me, "If you put your mind to do something, you can do it, but it takes a lot of hard work and dedication." As a kid, my hero was my father and my idol, Michael Jordan. At the time, Michael Jordan was a global icon. Jordan lead his Chicago Bulls franchise to six NBA championships, a two-time USA Olympic gold medal-winner, made his teammates better and showed people that he was the best player in the world. I wanted to be that guy!! I had the shoes, clothes, hat, the walk, even tried to chew gum like Mike.

After seeing the legendary Michael Jordan's success on the basketball court, I figured, why can't I play for the Chicago Bulls like him or even better. Growing up, I was fortunate to have a father working in a community center where I was able to access the basketball court, allowing me to fall in love with the game. As a child, my father had me play against older kids because that allowed me to prepare and gave me more advance experience than others my age. My father had travel teams during the summer. I always wanted to go with him and the team even though the kids were much older than me. That's how I fell in love with the game; I wanted to become a student of the game and figure out how to master my craft to become the best basketball player I could be. My father would work with me day and night and put his investment in my dreams. He told me, if you really want to make a career out of this, I'm going to teach you how to play the right way and learn the fundamentals. By fifth grade, I would dominate in the local leagues against kids my own age. I was the fastest player on the court, the tallest player, and I could handle the basketball better than most kids a few years older. That was a start of something special yet to come. One night, the junior high basketball coach, Dave Freberg, came by to watch me play; I was dominating the game, playing against middle school kids who were two to three years older than me; looking at me, he told my father "your son needs to tryout this season because he has a chance to become a special player." During my junior high playing experience, I was the first to average a triple double the whole season. It was unheard of at the time to see a kid average a triple double in junior high. That year, our team went 32-0 and won the Illinois state AA championship game by

BJHS Knights are the 8AA State Champs!
Team compiles a perfect 26-0 record

BJHS' 8th grade basketball team won the IESA Class 8AA State Championship on February 15 by beating Quincy 59-40, finishing a perfect 26-0 season. Over the course of two years, they compiled a record of 47-1. Members of the team included Steven Brown, Dylan Cook, Nate Dudley, Dodie Dunson, Brandon Holtz, Brent Holtz, Alex Rich, Delano Robinson, Ryan Strebing, Eric Trewett, and Wesley Ware.

more than 20 points. After the game, my teammate, Brandon Holtz, and I were invited to "The Real Deal All-Star Event" in Chicago, created by Coach Lewis Thorpe. Coach Thorpe held this event over 20 plus years to find the best basketball talent throughout the state of Illinois. It was time for me to put my skills to the test, now playing against supposedly the mecca of basketball with the intercity kids of Chicago. It has been proven over the years that there are a lot of talented players in Chicago who have gone on to play

15

in the NBA, overseas, and Division I colleges. With this reputation, I was a small-town guy trying to make a name for myself to prove that I was one the best basketball players in the state.

When I got to the gym, there were 40 plus kids playing in this event. A few of these players were highly skilled like Nate Minnoy (Purdue), Jerel McNeal (Marquette), DeAndre Thomas (Indiana), Tony Freeman (Iowa), Josh Tabb (Tennessee), Kevin Lisch (St. Louis) Jeremy Pargo (Gonzaga), Jamar Smith (Illinois), Brandon Ewing (Wyoming), Clarence Holloway (Louisville) and many more athletes. Around this time, two athletes really got most of the attention: Bobby Frazer who played at North Carolina and Julian Wright who played at Kansas, and who eventually went on to be drafted first round to the NBA by the New Orleans Pelicans.

The All-Star event was split up between the North vs. the South. The North had intercity players and the South had suburban or outside of the city athletes. The game was intense through all four quarters, and the pace was so fast. I was not used to playing against athletes who were bigger, stronger, and faster, and as competitive as I was at the same age. Our team pulled through in the end: The South won the game against the North 76 to 69. I had a good game, finishing with 23 points, dishing out 11 assists, with 5 steals, and walking away as the most valuable player. That day, my dad was a proud father who told me that the work that we were putting in everyday would one day lead to something special, possibly taking me places that I couldn't ever imagine.

2
High School
Knowing Yourself

"Watch your thoughts; they become words. Watch your words; they become actions. Watch your actions; they become habits. Watch your habits; they become character. Watch your character; it becomes your destiny."

— Lao Tzu

Chapter Two: High School – Knowing Yourself

During my freshman year, I made the varsity basketball team at Bloomington High School. Only a handful of players as freshmen made the varsity team in 30 years at Bloomington High before me and teammate, Brandon Holtz. Ron Rose was our head basketball coach who had played at Illinois Wesleyan University where he had led IWU to three NCAA Division III tournament appearances. He was 6th in the school history to assist as a player for the Titans. Playing at the high school level was a learning curve. I knew that I could compete with anyone but also understood that I had to earn my stripes as a player to get respect from the team. Coach Rose did not let me play much my first year because it was an adjustment from being a student athlete. I struggled with understanding the play book; the game was at a faster pace than middle school, and ultimately academically, things got difficult.

As a competitor, I challenged myself to improve in every aspect of my life, so that I could get back to what made me happy -- to be productive on the basketball floor. Coach Rose's guidance and leadership helped bring out the best in me and challenged me every day. If I trusted his philosophy, I had a chance to be part of something special that one day would lead our team to success. As a kid who had everything going in the direction of a competitor and the person I wanted to be, I've always had one weakness that I kept from everyone -- I was struggling with reading. Whenever I was called out to read in front of a crowd, I would get nervous because it was not my comfort place. I knew something was wrong, but I could never really figure out how to deal with these situations. My parents got me tested to see what they could do to help with my issue.

During the summer, going into my freshman year of high school, I was tested, I was diagnosed with a severe learning disability called, Development Reading Disorder (DRD), also known as dyslexia. Dyslexia is a reading disability that occurs when the brain doesn't properly recognize and process certain symbols. Dyslexia often runs through a family's genetics and can be passed down through generations. My disability was a combination of reading, developmental writing, and arithmetic. I struggled in classes and used to be made fun of because other kids would tell I couldn't read or spell, which put me in a quiet space. I would go home crying and was pretty hard on myself. Opening up to my parents helped me cope with my learning disability, and they continued to encourage me to make me feel more comfortable and confident every day I went back to school. By being diagnosed I was able to get special accommodations that would help me through my schooling. With this extra help, I knew that I did not have a normal brain like a regular student; I would have to study extra hard and longer hours to keep up with and understand my assignments. Even with these accommodations, I would get C's on exams, studying long hour, while a regular student could study in minutes and get an A. I just knew that I processed things differently.

I was in a combination regular and special educational class. The classes I excelled in were a breeze, but the classes that were challenging required extra assistance so I understood the material. Being in special educational classes, I felt somewhat out of place. The other students were physically capable of doing their assignments, but a majority had mental issues such as acting out as class clowns, becoming violent when things didn't go their way, and many needed special attention. I was embarrassed, not just about being in the class, but I would go home and see that my brother, who was two years younger, could do my homework better than me. I knew that the school was trying to put me in the best position to be successful and make things possible for a bright future. These classes helped built my self-confidence and a better mindset because I was learning a way not to be less of a human being. Starting off, things felt out of place, but after a few months in class, I realized that everyone learns differently and we all have a unique calling in life.

Going through freshman year of high school was a learning process -- learning how to deal with time management and academics, while playing basketball for the school team. Most of the time, I would show up late to basketball practice when I had to meet teachers after school to help catch up or learn tactics to process my studies better. Statistically as a freshman, I probably had the worse career year as a player since I had never played the game of basketball. I averaged less than 5 points and played less than 8 minutes a game. By the next year, I was determined and had the mindset to never, ever let that happen again.

The next summer I attended summer school and got caught up with academics, which allowed me to excel in basketball. Basketball was my life and an outlet that was my comfort zone. I was good at it and no one could judge me because I was better than the average person. That summer I lived in the gym. I wanted to prove to everyone that I was the best player on the team and could lead it to becoming the best in our league. My parents knew I was investing hours and days in the gym to improve my skills to become the best player I could be. It helped that I grew three inches in the summer, and my body started to fill out and develop. I would literally stay in the gym from 2 to 10 pm every night. While my friends would be doing other

activities such as swimming or playing video games, I was determined to be ahead of the game to prove a point. My mindset was, I'm going to have the best of both worlds, exceling in the classroom and on the court. During sophomore year, I made huge strides. With sacrifice and the hard work put in during the summer, by the time the season started, I finished as the team's leading scorer and rebounder and led the team in assists and steals all in the same season. I went from not playing at all the year before to becoming the starting point guard and co-captain. When all was said and done, through my high school playing career, I accomplished being a 3-time Illinois High School Association (IHSA) All-State basketball player, winning 3 straight intercity tournament champions and 2-time back to back Big 12 Conference championships, becoming Big 12 Conference Player of the Year and McDonalds All American Nominate; but the real highlight of my senior season was beating ESPN's nationally ranked #10 in the country and the state-ranked #2 Chicago Simeon Career Academy, led by Derrick Rose (NBA #1 Draft pick by the Chicago Bulls) in the Pontiac Holiday Classic tournament.

It was the first time in school history that Bloomington High School won the tournament, and I was Most Valuable Player of this prestige tournament. By the end of my high school season, I was blessed to receive over 20 Division I college basketball scholarships. I couldn't have done it without a great core of people who were positive influences around me, helping me create these opportunities. Sitting down with my parents for decision making, we felt so blessed because the ultimate goal was to use basketball to ultimately get a full-ride scholarship, so we would not have to pay for school; God made it happen. I was very blessed and humbled, but putting in the work and chasing the dream to play college basketball was the mission.

"Statistically there are over 550,000 student athletes that play high school basketball in the United States. Only 0.9% of high school basketball players compete at the NCAA Division I level on scholarship, Scholarshipsstats.com."

2,019 Schools sponsored varsity Basketball programs in 2017:

Division	# of Schools	# of teams Men's	Women's	Total Athletes Men	Women	Average team size Men's	Women's	# of Scholarships limit per team Men	Women	Average Athletic Scholarship * Men	Women
NCAA I	351	351	349	5,522	5,588	16	16	13	15	16,154	17,114
NCAA II	314	311	312	5,251	4,826	17	15	10	10	6,329	7,650
NCAA III	446	425	442	7,767	6,675	18	15	-	-	-	-
NAIA I	99	95	98	1,864	1,549	20	16	11	11	7,329	7,762
NAIA II	133	133	133	2,752	2,208	21	17	6	6	5,353	5,626
Other 4 year	99	96	81	1,394	916	15	11	-	-	470	609
NJCAA	431	425	386	6,352	4,910	15	13	15	15	2,479	3,002
Other 2 year	146	141	137	1,988	1,633	14	12	-	-	259	384
Totals	2,019	1,977	1,938	32,890	28,305	17	15			5,166	5,731

"NCAA I basketball is a headcount sport, so the athletic scholarship limits of 13 for men and 15 for women are the limit; NCAA II basketball is an equivalency sport and partial scholarships can be awarded to meet the limit per school, so an NCAA II school could award 15 players each a 2/3 equivalent scholarship and meet the limit of 10 per team. (See our page on scholarship limits for more information, Scholarshipstatics.com.")

"Average athletic scholarship is the average amount of athletically related student aid per athlete for All varsity sports sponsored by the school. Some athletes receive full awards, some receive partial and many receive none. Additionally, some sports within a school may be fully funded, some partially and some sports provide no athletic scholarships. Private schools generally have higher tuition than public schools and the average award will reflect this, Odds of high school athletes playing college."

Close friends who played basketball made decisions early on and knew where they were going; my close teammate, Brandon Holtz, decided to attend Illinois State University. After watching him sign, he would mention to me that it would be nice to play together in college after having had a great high school career together. Evaluating the proposition and sitting down with my parents to make the decision was difficult. We ultimately came to the decision for me to stay local and sign with Illinois State University. But by the end of the summer, I did what was in my best interest and did not attend the University; but rather Prep School. I got a lot of heat from people in town who were not happy with my decision. Some thought it was a selfish move, but there were multiple factors that played into the decision. I knew the history of Illinois State University as a great institution because my mother and grand-mother had graduated from there, but it was not best for me at the time, I made a decision that would change my life forever.

3
Prep School
Creating Opportunities

"Listen to the rhythm of your own calling, and follow that."

- Oprah Winfrey

Chapter Three: Prep School Creating Opportunities

During this time of my life, I made the decision to attend Brewster Academy (BA) in Wolfeboro, New Hampshire. BA is a co-educational independent boarding school with roughly 400 students from grade 9th through 12th as well as post graduates. The school covers over 80 acres of land and occupies on 0.5 miles (800 m) of shoreline among Lake Winnipesaukee. This lake is the third-largest in the New England area. The lake contains at least 258 islands.

Moving to New Hampshire was culture shock. I can remember it like it was yesterday. My parents and brother drove me from Illinois to New Hampshire, and it took us almost 18 hours by car. Making this decision really helped me academically; due to a post-graduate year, it was like

getting a fifth year of high school. This extra year, didn't affect my college athletic clock, but a few classes I took counted towards college credit. The decision to bag out of my commitment was tough, but being far away from family was even tougher. Being away from home for the first time was a learning experience: meeting new friends, being able to juggle my time, and undergoing many more new aspects of my life. It wasn't tough making new friends, but a majority of the students were well off economically in the higher financial class.

These kids were driving Hummers, Range Rovers, Lexus, Mercedes Benz, Jaguars, and all types of fancy expensive vehicles. When I got to campus, the first student

I met was Daniel Vlasic from Detroit, Michigan. When I introduced myself, he knew exactly who I was because Danial was a sports fanatic, but I felt kind of bad because I didn't know him. After a few general conversations, Daniel told me that his grandpa had started the Vlasic business. Vlasic is known for pickles sold nationwide. I lived in Bearce Residence Hall, which was a house. I had roommates from all different parts of the country. Brian Grimes was from Philadelphia, Pennsylvania Will Harris was from Brooklyn, New York, Ryan Blickle was from Mauldin, South Carolina, and Will Riley was from Boston, Massachusetts. We lived on bunk beds and the house was so old that some days we thought that it would cave in and fall on us. Meeting new people and learning about different backgrounds helped me understand various cultures. The head basketball coach, Jason Smith, took a chance on signing his second player ever from the state of Illinois. Coach Smith heard that I was a talented player and we talked over the phone; he told me his expectations and said, you're going to have to make an adjustment in a new environment. I told Coach Smith I would do whatever it took to contribute in the best interests of the team and to put myself in a position to do well academically and on the court. Coach Smith knew we had a

pretty good team because a majority of the team were already signed to play Division I college basketball after the season. Every day in open gym, we would have college coaches coming from all over the country.

Coach Smith told all of us before the season, if we win, we would all benefit from the team's success. He believed that everyone had an opportunity to play at the college basketball level and possibly get a free education. During my prep school season, I started every single game and averaged 17 points, 4 assists, 4 rebounds per game, leading our team to 20-9 record and a top 5 national ranking in the country.

I was ranked in the top graduate players of 2006 by Scout.com and Hoopscoop.com recruiting services. My recruiting skyrocketed and I was getting interest and offers from conferences ranging from the Big 12, Big Ten, Big East, Pac 12, and many mid major programs. Recruiting became overwhelming because college scouts were seeing a difference in my ability in basketball that they never had seen before. Getting the extra help academically and succeeding in the classroom really translated to the court and helped me be get back on the top of my game. By the end of the season, I narrowed my recruiting list down to five schools. These five schools really stood out due to the history of their programs: University of Iowa, University of

Minnesota, Iowa State University, Northern Illinois University, and University of Tulsa. All these schools had great traditions, but I had to find what suited me academically. After making a few visits, the one that most interest me was Iowa State University. I set up a visit, and at the time Coach Greg McDermott had just gotten a job. He recruited me out of high school when he was the head basketball coach at Northern Iowa University. The ISU coaching staff showed me around and sat me down to talk about where they saw me in their future plans. With a few of ISU's guards deciding to leave early to play professionally, it gave me an opportunity to play; and, academically, it seemed they had the resources to help me succeed. As the final day wrapped up, they made a scholarship offer; and I felt that it was just right. After talking to my close circle, I made the decision to commit to Iowa State University. It was a tough race between all of the institution, but one had to be chosen.

4

College
Self-Motivation

"One thing we can all control is effort. Put in the time to become an expert in whatever you're doing."

— Mark Cuban

Chapter Four: College – Self-Motivation

Iowa State University

This was an exciting year for me. Being away from home for the second time around became a lot easier and I became more independent. I was going in clueless as to how things would pan out, but I knew it would be a great start to my college career. The first day stepping on campus, I realized how big the institution was -- no joke. There were just under 36,500 students; the campus contains over 160 buildings and features 490 acres of trees, plants and classically-designed buildings. Being on this campus when school was in session was unbelievable.

I bonded with people I would consider as life-long friends. My roommates were Corey Johnson, Wesley Johnson, and Mike Taylor. We were all unique in our own ways, where we came from how we were the best players for our team. We all came in as freshman besides Mike -- he came from a powerhouse junior college in Florida. At our first meeting with the coaching staff and Coach McDermott, we learned that he was very strict about doing things the right way. Coach McDermott kept it short with four rules:

Rule #1:"Be on time"
Rule #2: "Be Accountable for yourself and your teammates"
Rule #3:"Work hard and take care of your business off the floor"
Rule #4:"Don't lie"

These four principals helped me shape into the person I am today. These rules correlate with helping us as athletes become responsible and accountable young men. Coach McDermott was big on team chemistry and believed that playing all of us would help win basketball games. He never showed favoritism and always had an open-door policy. As freshman playing against older players, we played with a chip on our shoulders because we had to prove that we belonged.

I struggled academically during the beginning of the season but I was able to get special assistance by the men's and women's academic advisor, Jeff Cesler. Jeff helped me keep me spirts lifted and told me that I was not the only person struggling in the classroom. He promised that the school would help me succeed if I put the time and energy into my academics. I listened to everything he told me to do and thus saw improvements in my academic success. I was never afraid of putting in the work; I just needed someone to help me learn in a way I could understand the assignment and information. Jeff and I worked hand-in-hand doing extra hours during his off time. For him to work with me beyond his working hours was a true blessing. Jeff put in time, energy and effort and made an investment in me when he didn't have to. Without him at ISU, I would have never made it on the basketball floor. As I continued to do well in the classroom, my production on the court increased.

College basketball was at an all-time high and very competitive that season. I played against three out of the top four picks in the 2007 picks in the NBA draft. In the basketball Big 12 Conference were superstars on the rise. At the time, the conference was rated as the one that had the most talented individual basketball players. Playing against arguably the best college athletes in the world, we were battle tested. We finished the season with a 17-16 record and 6-10 in the conference. I played in all 31 games, averaging 5.2 points and 1.5 rebounds per game, leading the team in the free-throw percentage and was ranked top 25 in the NCAA Division I. I was ranked fourth in school history for the most three-pointer field goals made by a freshman. I was fortunate to play for a coach who believed in my ability as a freshman because most freshman around the country did not play this many minutes. By the end of

41

the season, it was a struggle for me academically, but things were working very well on the basketball court. Academically, I got to the border line of becoming academically ineligible. I sat down at the end of the year with Coach McDermott who told me, you have to weigh all your pros and cons for next season. I told him I was on the fence about leaving or staying due to my academic struggle and personal reasons. As the head coach, he wanted me to return but understood that I might not come back. I decided not to return to ISU, as academically, they had done all they could do to lessen my struggles, but the day-to-day productivity became hard and I was overwhelmed. In the end, they made sure that I was academically eligible to transfer anywhere I wanted.

After leaving, I thanked coach McDermott and the coaching staff for giving me an opportunity to be a part of a special family with all the life lessons and encouragement of a support system. To this day, Coach McDermott contacts me on my birthday and every Christmas to see how things are going. Coach McDermott is one classy guy, even though I was not a player anymore in the program. When I left ISU, everyone I had come in with did not stay. Cory Johnson transferred to Valparaiso University and currently is playing professional overseas in Spain; Mike Taylor was dismissed from the ISU program due to personal issues and continues to pursue his basketball dreams by playing in the G-League. Mike became the first person to be drafted to the NBA out of the minor leagues and Wesley transferred to Syracuse University and became a bigtime superstar. Wesley was drafted as the #4 pick in the NBA to the Minnesota Timberwolves. At the end of the day, people make decisions on what is best with their future success.

Vincennes University
It was a tough decision to leave ISU, but I knew that if I were going to have the best of both worlds as a student athlete, I needed to go the junior college route. I called a long-time friend who had spent over two decades within the sport. His name was Jerry Mullens. Jerry has created a

national brand for more than 25 years with colleges and universities. Jerry provides them with the most accurate and complete information about the nation's top junior college, prep, and high school basketball players. His scouting services and high-profile events are among the most respected and anticipated in men's basketball. We talked about my situation and he gave me some advice about what could be helpful. Jerry knew everyone in the junior college rankings and that day when I left ISU, colleges would recruit me heavily. I had to find a school where I could get a quality education, have an opportunity to compete for a championship, and also participate in a program that would have my best interests at heart.

Narrowing my list down was easy, and I choose to go to Vincennes University (VU) in Indiana. VU is the oldest public institution of higher learning in the state. With its tradition of winning success, it has been considered a powerhouse program for many generations in junior college athletics. The head basketball coach was Everick Sullivan.

Coach Sullivan played at the University of Louisville under the legendary Denny Crum. At Louisville, the coach took his team to three NCAA tournaments and held all-time records in the school history in scoring, three-point percentages, dunks, and assists. Coach Sullivan also played eight years professionally overseas before he broke the coaching ranks. It was very intriguing for me to play for a coach who had been there and done it before. With guidance, Coach Sullivan believed that he could help me reach my full potential and also help bring VU success.

Jerry invited me to the National Junior College Showcase. The Top 50 basketball junior college players in the country were at the camp. The camp was in Tulsa, Oklahoma; and when I got there, I was among the best of the best at the junior college level. The competition was really good. Most players were in the same situation as I was in -- there to showcase their talent to get exposure to hopefully continue their careers at a four-year university. Most of these players were better than some that I had played against when I attended ISU. By the end of the event, I blew the tournament out of the water. Tons of college scouts were impressed with my game and told me and Coach Sullivan that they would be in touch throughout the season. A few Division I programs offered me scholarships before I even started my first game. I had one year before going back to the Division I level and knew that whenever I made my decision, I had to make it count.

Before the season started, my grandmother passed away. She had been battling cancer most of her life, but the past few years really took a toll. I was blessed to have known her while she was alive. It really hit me hard because we were very close. In anything I ever wanted to accomplish, she always told me to "never give up" in what I wanted to do or who I wanted to become. It was great to have teammates and a coaching staff that supported me and was there for me around this difficult time. Right then and there, being a student athlete meant much more to me. It was like a light switch flipped, and I now wanted to do something bigger. I made a promise to that I was going to challenge myself and share my story with anyone who believed in their own dream.

My academics went very well, and I felt that a smaller college benefit me. The smaller class sizes allowed me to learn better and also have the individual attention I needed with academic tutors. I joined an academic program called Student Transition into Educational Program (STEP). Robyn Dragger was an academic advisor for this program. Robyn took me under her wing and was instrumental in teaching me how to speak up and ask questions. She taught me how to get outside my comfort zone and challenge myself to expand my mind and knowledge in the classroom. Her favorite line was, "Dunson, you have a special story to share; don't let yourself become unknown." Hence, the creation of this story. "Unknown Student Athlete."

The STEP program provided comprehensive services for Learning Disabilities (LD) students in the university mainstream. It was designed to help students be more successful in their college courses by having a specialist for individualized tutoring sessions. The first time I attended a class, there were on average 15-20 students, which was awesome. At Iowa State University, I would have anywhere from 80-130 students in big lecture halls. The VU professors would encourage most of the students to speak their minds if they did not know the answer to a question. After Robyn's comment, I felt right at home and there was a sense of comfort. Going through my academic year at VU, I continued to build self- confidence and knew that when it was time to graduate, I would be ready for the next chapter of my life. We had a talented basketball team. We had players who were good but a few were immature. Most came to prove they were better than the players who had transferred in from different schools. The returning players were competitive and felt that they were the best players on the team, and no one would step on their territory.

We were all intelligent and unique in our own ways. At the beginning of the season, we were ranked one of the top 10 teams in the National Junior College Athletic Association (NJCAA). Coach Sullivan made me team captain because of my leadership qualities, and I was honored to lead the team. I told the coach and the players that every player was a captain. That's always been my model; it's never about what can I do to help the team. I understood that there are individual accolades to be made, but without the team, success doesn't happen for anyone. My parents raised me to be a servant of God. I never worry about my individual self; I always played for the person next to me and to do everything through God's will. Coach

49

Sullivan believed that we had enough talent to be good, but if we had the right chemistry and stayed healthy, we could make a run for the national championship. Everyone on our team had the ability to play at a four-year institution after junior college, but were we willing to make the sacrifice. I led VU to a 28-6 record, and we were undefeated at home the whole season, going 16-0. We were ranked #3 in NJCAA polls and earned a NJCAA National Tournament appearance. Getting to the tournament, we fell short against Salt Lake City Community College (SLCC). We led at half time, but we didn't have a great showing against a team we felt we were better than. SLCC went on that year to win the National Championship. After a successful season, almost every player moved to a four-year university to continue their education and also play basketball on a full scholarship. Going through the whole recruiting process was great, but at the same time I knew whatever institution I chose, this would be my last stop. Being recruited by Division I schools ranging from mid to high major level weighed on me heavily. Narrowing it down to the next school became easier because I'd been down this path a couple times.

My top two schools were Bradley University (BU) and Indiana University (IU). There were more schools in the mix, but these two programs had personal connections for; I could see myself in a position to become successful. The two schools both had great academics resources to help accommodate me with my learning disability. Looking at both, one team was in the Big Ten Conference while the other was in the Missouri Valley Conference. An opportunity to compete for a team championship? Class size smaller or bigger? Good distance or closer to home? These thoughts were going through my head. Tom Crean had just left Marquette University to take the head coach job at IU. Coach Crean had a lot of success producing and developing players like Dwayne Wade. With his new program, Coach Crean was in the rebuilding stage in which he felt that things were going to take time; that's how it should be.

I respected Coach Crean because he always put his players first and challenged them to become the best they could be on and off the basketball court. Taking a visit to Bradley University, I met head coach, Jim Les. Coach Les had known me since my high school days and had recruited me as early as the eighth grade. When my family and I arrived on campus, Coach Les and the coaching staff laid out the red carpet and welcomed us with open arms. We talked about how I would fit into the basketball system because of the similarities he saw in me; he already knew as a former Bradley brave and NBA player. I love the fact that he had played the game before and had a good understanding of what I was trying to do to impact a program. Coach Les had played seven seasons in the NBA, from 1988 to 1995 for four different franchise teams. He was the first coach to offer me a full scholarship when I was a freshman in high school. I remember when I had to give him the terrible news that I was going to another university. Coach Les showed how much of a classy guy he was and his character. He mentioned how important academics were and getting a quality education, and believed if I had the right opportunity, I could play at the professional level. When I left Bradley University, I knew they would have a plan in place, and I waited only a week to make my decision. All the questions from both institutions had been answered and I prayed about it with my family, because I knew this would be the final chapter of my college basketball life. That Sunday morning, I decided to call Coach Les and commit to Bradley University.

Bradley University

I felt that by going to BU, I had a chance to reach my full potential along with the returning players and the new additions. The transition from VU to BU went pretty smoothly. Positive vibes were coming towards me and I knew the BU tradition from past history. Being less than 40 miles from my hometown made it nice. It would be easy for family and friends to come and see me play. When my teammates and I would go into the community, to the grocery store, and attend different events, people would come up to speak with us about the upcoming season. They were looking forward to attending home games and see the team play. The community was very serious about their basketball because it was the biggest show in town. Not having a college football team, basketball at BU fans from all over. Coach Les would tell us every time we left campus, "You are always in the public eye." He was right about that. The local people in town watched everything we did; so how we carried ourselves was important to the image of our program and its reputation. We did things the right way and wanted to represent our university with pride and dignity.

Attending my first summer school session at BU, I did very well and was able to manage the classes I took. With the academic advisor's game plan, they made sure that going into the fall semester that I had a plan in place. The academic advisors believed in planning ahead and made sure that I had every resource possible to make the transition better. Coach Les immediately arranged for a personal tutor to work with me daily. I could only use the tutor within the guidelines of my learning disability accommodations. I felt that God had answered my prayers when they made the decision to have a tutor who could help me learn by teaching me different ways to study. During this time, the school was making a transition by hiring a new wave of employees in the athletic department. The school hired an assistant academic coordinator to help the head coordinator. To juggle so many athletes, it really helped multiple sports to have another full-time academic coordinator to spread over all the men's and women's teams. BU hired Heather Moles. Today Heather is like a mother to me. When the institution hired her, they hired an employee who could relate to students because she was previously a former student athlete. Heather played field hockey at Duke University, she still holds the Blue Devil record for career saves. Heather could relate to how difficult and over whelming things can get in college, but she believed that no challenge was impossible. We spent time studying one-on-one to better prepare me for my classes. She would commend me for dedicating my time and energy and not giving up on academics. I would spend most of my free time on the weekends studying. While my teammates spent their weekends partying, having a good time or sleeping, I would be studying by myself. Heather was a blessing, if I needed additional help with my studies she would accommodate and would make sure we met. There were times when I would have morning exams and we would meet Heather at the academic success office to review my study material. A typical day for me at BU during the week was: get up early to meet with Heather over academics, go to practice, study, go to class, get treatment or extra basketball time to improve my basketball game, then study before the night was over. Then the next day, do the same thing all over again for three years. I would spend at least 20-30 hours a week in acidic services depending on what I had to get done with my assignments. She made school less challenging by breaking down assignments in a way I could understand.

My junior season at BU, I was elected team co-captain in my first season before I even played in a game. Coach Les thought I brought to practice energy every day but respected how hard I played on the court. The first game of the season, I opened with a breakout game at

home, scoring 21 points in a tough win over the University of Illinois Chicago. The first week of my college basketball career, I was

named Missouri Valley Conference Newcomer of the Week. Throughout the season, we had a roller coaster ride, but finished with a 22-14 record and lost in conference postseason semi-finals against the University Northern Iowa. We were two games away from making the NCAA tournament. We were invited to the post season to play in the College Insider Tournament (CIT). Before the tournament, Coach Les knew that I had broken my hand a few games back. We sat down and talked; he told me, "you can make a choice to play or end the season before the tournament. Head athletic trainer, Dr. Marcus Ohnemus, told me he was out of options for me after a few cortisone shots in my hand due to a broken bone; but said, "If you play, you're going to have a lot of pain or you can sit it out the rest of the season?" Nothing was going to stop me from sitting out. Today, looking at the situation, it might not have been a wise choice for me to play; but if I had to do it all over again, I would do it the same way. After the first game in the CIT tournament, we went on to win against Austin Peay at home.

After the game, my hand looked like the size of a tennis ball. Our team advanced to the sweet 16, and my teammate, Chris Roberts, made a 75-footer buzzer beater shot with 3.3 seconds left to save our season so we could advance to the CIT final four. We then turned around days later to play the University of Pacific and won at home 59-49. We had a week to prepare for Old Dominion University in the championship game. Our bodies were banged up and a few players including me had injuries, but we knew that we had a shot to compete for the championship. Overall, we fought a good game and came up short, losing 62-66. For an injury-prone team, we made huge strides and learned that when a team comes together at the right time, special things happen. Going into my senior season, I got my body into the best possible physical shape by getting bigger, stronger, and faster to finish my career on top. During the first few weeks of practice, Coach Les was impressed with my mindset and how I would lead by example for our team. The second game of the season, we were playing Idaho State University at home. I had a dominant scoring performance in the first half of the game leading with 16 points in only 12 minutes of action on the floor. That night, it was one of those nights when every shot felt like it was going into the hoop. My teammates were encouraging and the coaching staff at half time told everyone, "Dodie is feeling it on the offensive end of the floor; keep getting him the basketball". Every night someone would be performing at their best, and that happened to me that night.

The start of the second half, I caught the basketball on the left side wing and passed my opponent on the wing to the basket, going in for a dunk. In mid-air, I was accidently undercut, and while coming down, I landed on my forearm. I couldn't feel my fingers or my arm. Quickly, my arm went numb and the athletic trainer ran onto the court to see if I was okay. When the referees told the players to go to the benches, I knew something was wrong.

Dr. Ohnemus knew that I had broken something because during the fall, there was a loud popping noise. The moment of the injury, I asked myself, "Why me, God? Why does it have to be me? Security and a few athletic trainers helped me get back to the locker room. When I looked down at my forearm, my bones were broken in half, and barely connected. I've never been in so much pain in my life. I cried for the next few days, knowing that my basketball career could be over. With confirmation from Dr. Ohnemus, the NCAA granted me a medical hardship, which would allow me to come back and play for a fifth year. After hearing this news, all I could do was smile, but nothing mattered until I met with the doctor. After a painful few hours, the doctors took x-rays of my forearm to see how bad the accident was. When the doctor came back with the x-rays, he told me in his exact words, "We have good news and bad news. First the good news. You are alive and you're going to live. The bad news is that I can't guarantee you that you will be able to play basketball again." My forearm injury could have been the equivalent of a bad car accident. I broke both of my bones in my arm and was broken up into multiple pieces. I was in shock! In disbelief, I exclaimed to the doctor that this can't happen. I never cheated the game when working in the gym behind closed doors .I spent so much time and investment in putting myself in a position to become the best athlete I could be for our team -- late nights in the gym, and improving my game to help lead our basketball program. I was born to play this game. I sat down and cried because all of the blood, sweat, and tears was going to waste. At that moment, I got down on one knee and started praying. I called friends, other family members, and told people who didn't even know me to pray for me. All I could do was leave everything in the Lord's hands. The doctor gave me time to cope and all I could do was pray. Knowing I only had a 50% chance to ever play again was tough, but at the end of the day, I knew I had to accept the odds. But I believed I was going to get through surgery and the Lord was with me the whole time. After a successful six-hour surgery, it was miracle!! I could bend my fingers and arm!! I knew the Lord had answered my prayers. The doctor showed me where they made cuts to put my forearm bones back together. Today, I have a huge scar on both sides of the forearm and also two metal plates with over sixty metal screws that will hold my arm in place for the rest of my life. After checking out of the hospital, I knew the road for a comeback would be a long process, but I was ready to get back and attack the grind.

After four to five weeks, I was allowed to do rehab and was excited and anxious at the same time. Meeting with the Dr. Ohnemus, he told me, "I will help you get back to where you need to be, but if you work hard at it, we can make your forearm even stronger than before. It will be painful, but just know it will all pay off in the end." If I believed in anyone I would believe Dr. Ohnemus. He was a man of his word, I'd never been through so much pain as going through rehab. My typical day was waking up, studying, rehab, class, rehab, study, rehab in practice, class, and then more rehab late after the building had closed. I would do that for weeks and months until I was cleared to play. By the end of the year, Dr. Ohnemus got me back in shape and I felt better than ever.

Going into my 5th year of college, I was so ahead in my academics that I could have graduated going into the fall semester of my fifth year in college. My academic advisors advice was to spread my class schedule out so I wouldn't have a heavy load during the fall and spring semesters. Knowing that I was on track to graduate was a blessing and being around people who encouraged me every day and wanted me to succeed was a further blessing. During the basketball season, things started to change in a different direction. We had a few coaching changes and a young inexperienced team, with a few veteran players hurt. We had a rollercoaster season. We started off the season winning our first four games; then our team would hit road blocks, losing close games to teams we usually beat. By the time the Missouri Valley Conference season started, we had showed our inexperience as a team, but we would never give up or throw in the towel. We believed in fighting to the very end. Even though we did not have the season we had imagined, I felt that I was able to mentor our younger teammates and groom them for their future basketball careers. I felt most times like a player-coach in practice, teaching basic drills while leading by example, playing hard and being a student of the game. At the end of the season, a majority of the players thanked me for helping make them better on and off the court to help prepare them for their futures. Looking back at my playing career, I experienced a lot of adversity through good times and bad. Making sacrifices, showing determination and self-motivation were the keys principles that helped shape my life. As a kid being told you're not smart enough, and not being able to get through school, I proved people wrong. One thing I learned is that even though I had a learning disability it did not stop me from becoming the person I wanted to be and who the person I could become. Even though my life has taken me through many ups and downs there has been no doubt that I have achieved my ultimate goal which was graduating from college and getting my degree.

5

Dunson's
Key Principles

"Everyone learns differently, but finding a way that best fits your learning style is the key to individual success."

– Dodie Dunson II

Chapter Five: Dunson's Key Principles

After telling my story, I've learned a few things through my experience. The key principles that have helped me succeed.

Invest in Yourself

As a kid, I believed that one day I would become a college basketball student athlete. At a very young age, I would spend a lot of time working on my craft to become the best basketball player I could be and earn an opportunity to become an elite athlete. I was fortunate to have parents who invested in me, and with the extra push and support, they helped me reach one of my goals.

Trust the Process

Believe in yourself when no one is watching or putting in the work before anything happens. I was a firm believer in creating opportunities before things were presented to me. By preparing, it allowed me to be ready before the opportunity came. To be successful, you have to put the work in.

Become a Sponge

My parents and mentors have prepped me on becoming a life-long learner. Every day, I continue to learn something new to shape my journey to success. The more you continue to learn, the more knowledge you have. The more educated you become you become an expert in your own future to create your own path to prepare the next generation.

Plan Long-Term Goals

As a kid, I believed in dreaming big. I continue to challenge myself daily to become a better version of myself. Setting future goals allows me to plan for the future and give me the opportunity to be my own success.

Understanding the Meaning of a Work-Life Balance

As a husband, I balance my career and personal life. At the same time, I continue to keep God first and continue to pursue my dreams and goals without having to sacrifice the time spent with my family. As we continue on in life, I will prepare the future foundation for my children and teach the key principles that have helped me succeed.

Made in the USA
Columbia, SC
20 January 2020